A
Mystical
Heart

Edwina Gateley

A Mystical Heart

52 Weeks in the Presence of God

with illustrations by the author

A Crossroad Book
The Crossroad Publishing Company
New York

The Crossroad Publishing Company
370 Lexington Avenue, New York, NY 10017

Printed in the United States of America

Library of Congress Cataloging-in-Publication Data

Gateley, Edwina.
    A mystical heart : fifty-two weeks in the presence of God /
Edwina Gateley.
        p.   cm.
    Includes bibliographical references.
    ISBN 0-8245-1764-4 (pbk.)
    1. Mysticism. 2. Spiritual life.   I. Title.
BL625.G35   1998
242′.2 – dc21   98-22227

4   5   6   7   8   9   10   02   01

*For the Benedictine Sisters of Erie, Pennsylvania,
who provide me with a place to write and a constant embrace
of love, friendship, and support.*

*Also for the women of Sophia's Circle, Chicago,
who have dedicated themselves to raising funds
to create places of nurturing and healing for women
to get in touch with their mystical hearts.*

Acknowledgments

This book has been written because of a small group of women whose faith in my ability to write and whose constant affirmation and support during its difficult birthing made it become a reality.

I would like to thank Sr. Jean Lavin, OSB, who was a wonderful listener and reader for this book; Sr. Miriam Mashank, OSB, who gave unwavering affirmation; Sr. Susan Freitag, OSB, who left me awed with her computer and layout skills; Carolyn Vogt Groves, Ed Goerz, and Henry Fischer for their research and suggestions; and Maureen Donnelly, who took care of child, pets, and home while I hid in the woods to write.

Introduction

THROUGHOUT HUMAN HISTORY mystics and prophets have arisen, particularly in times of oppression and fear, to comfort God's people and assure them of God's presence and love. This book offers a contemporary reflection on the mystical and prophetic voice that has articulated the divine presence at the heart of human activity throughout history. It is written to remind us that God is present, and always has been, and that we are invited to recognize God's presence through the voices and experiences of men and women whose lives and deep love for God and for others are a testimony to divine inspiration, grace, and constancy.

In our world today there is a tangible apprehension that affects all of us. We know that all is not well. We know that we are not a just and holy people. We know that in many ways we have failed to reflect the face of God — to build a world of justice, peace, and equality. This consciousness can so leave us victims of our own despair and failure that our lives come to embody fear and therefore faithlessness. Deep down we begin to suspect that we will never really make it — that we will never, after all, be able to open ourselves to personal and global transformation. Deep down the seeds of despair slowly take root as we confront a world of increasing violence, hostility, and hunger. Our hearts sink. This book invites us to allow our hearts to sink into God that we may through that very faith-filled fall come to rise up in hope.

This book is written to renew our dreams and rekindle our faith, for it is into the very midst of our trembling world that the voice of the mystic and the prophet breaks through with a powerful message of hope and challenge. "The Mystical Heart" reminds us not only that God is still very much with us, but that God has expectations of us and that, even more importantly, we are capable of fulfilling them in spite of the chaos of our world and the breaking open of our hearts.

It is, in fact, the breaking open of our hearts that precipitates the moment of conversion from a timid heart to a mystical heart. At that precise breaking point we come to know that God is with us and that new life is possible even in the midst of despair. This is the transformative experience of real faith. It is this kind of personal and deep faith in God and in each other which will lead us to become healed and therefore to become healers. It is the conversion from hearts of stone to hearts of flesh.

The voice of the mystic tells us who we are and what we are capable of. That voice is here with us. It always has been. But perhaps today, more than ever, it needs to be heard. Now, more than ever in human history, we trembling, fearful people need to know that we each have, deep within us, the mystical heart. And no matter how little we may actually *feel* God's presence, the mystical heart knows that it is there — an everlasting and constant presence urging us to be comforted and to trust.

Like a shadow, God clings to us, ever nudging us to deeper awareness and new life — toward the dream of rebuilding ourselves and our world. It is this certainty of God's presence within us and around us, soaked in all things, that leaves us comforted, reassured, and affirmed. We are invited to listen to our own mystical heart. In doing so we come to understand how deeply we are loved. We are awed and grateful.

Mysticism is not
an acquired or learned thing;
it is not a matter
of studying form or content.

Mysticism is a negation,
an emptying out
of dreams and plans and
anxieties that bind the spirit.

Mysticism is that state
of living in, and embracing
the immediate and the now
in utter naked faith.

Mysticism is the whispered yes
as we tremble before
that which we do not understand
nor control, yet we desire.

Mysticism is daily assent
to all,
a mighty offering up
of existence.

A Mystical Heart

Week 1

The soul is the greening life force [viriditas] of the flesh,
for the body grows and prospers through her,
just as the earth becomes fruitful when it is moistened.
The soul humidifies the body so it does not dry out,
just like the rain which soaks into the earth.

— HILDEGARD OF BINGEN

Today,
as if the sky has fallen,
a wet mist hangs
over the earth
drenching all in moisture,
swelling dried-up things
into heaviness,
impregnating little seeds
and shifting soil and grasses.

Ah, today,
so does God's grace
hover over the earth
like a great dew
caressing our dried-up spirits
and seeping imperceptibly
into our souls,

14

rising them
into pregnancy.

Ah, today,
God, ever expectant,
gently and patiently strokes
the embryonic waters
we fearfully guard within,
dreaming of,
longing for
the great Breaking Open,
the bursting of new life.

This Week:

Plant something.

Week 2

When the student is ready,
the teacher will come.

—EASTERN SAYING

We are so hungry!
There is such a deep unmet longing in us
that we are driven to erratic and anxious enrollments
in seminars, retreats, and workshops
on myriad themes of spirituality, healing, wholeness,
and even miracle making!

Millions of us are searching for a spiritual jumpstart
or an instant divine fix.
But our journey begins in spiritual infancy
and unfolds and grows
through our everyday life experiences.
It is all right to be hungry.
It is all right to want more.
But it is God who feeds the waiting heart.
We must be empty vessels,
not afraid of that very emptiness.
We must wait –
ever gentle with ourselves –
until God scoops us up, and comforts us.

This Week:

Just be exactly where you are –
it is where you are meant to be.
Rejoice in it.

Week 3

Be comforted.
You would not be seeking me,
if you had not already found me.

— BLAISE PASCAL

I do not need
to seek God.
God is already here
waiting to be found,
soaked in my reality.
My journey is to be one
of recognizing God,
always,
already present,
and surfacing
that presence in
my daily life.

This Week:

Close your eyes.
Breathe deeply
and imagine yourself
soaked in God.

Week 4

Just to be is a blessing.
Just to live is holy.
—ABRAHAM JOSHUA HESCHEL

Often we seek God
in all the wrong places.
It would be better
if we didn't look at all,
if we would allow ourselves
to dare to believe
that it is God's delight
to simply gaze upon us;
that God, who birthed us
in a great burst of passion,
is ever standing by in waiting,
longing to catch our attention,
endlessly hoping
that we might be startled
into recognition
as we wander lazily by
the radiant primrose –
snuggled in the grass.

This Week:

Enjoy the flowers.

Week 5

Cultivate stillness.
Breathe harmony.
Become tranquillity.
As the ten thousand things
rise and fall, rise and fall,
just witness their return to the root.
—THE TAO TE CHING OF LAO TZU

Whatever happens to me in life
I must believe that somewhere,
in the mess or madness of it all,
there is a sacred potential –
a possibility for wondrous redemption
in the embracing of all that is.
For in the unfolding of my journey,
in all its soaring delight
and crushing pain,
I may be sure that God is there –
always ahead, behind, below, and above,
encompassing all that befalls me
in a circle of deep compassion.
And there,
above the darkness

that wraps me round
the bright wings of the Dove
hover and beat
in gentle healing love
and invitation to
New Rising.

This Week:

**Be patient and accepting
of whatever is happening
in your life right now.
There will be meaning.**

Week 6

This is a time to cry out.
One is ashamed to be human.
One is embarrassed to be called religious
in the face of religious failure
to keep alive the image of God
in the face of humanity. . . .
We have imprisoned God
in our temples and slogans,
and now the Word of God
is dying on our lips.

—ABRAHAM JOSHUA HESCHEL

God, I believe,
wants to surprise us,
for God hides in the world
hoping to be discovered.
But we, fixed on
our own sacred imaginings,
clutching our icons
and performing perfectly
our sacred rituals,
trample, unseeing,
on the holy beneath our feet,
and pass by, not minding,

the blank-eyed crowds
milling all around us
unrecognized,
longing to be discovered,
longing to be surprised.
God – longing to be uttered.

This Week:

Sit in the shopping mall,
or in any busy place,
and, prayerfully, allow yourself
to recognize God's presence
in the people you see.

Week 7

My experience of emptiness
is that it is alive
with the possibility
of everything waiting to be born.

— MARTIN MARTY

In the crying of the wind,
oh, speak to me, my God,
for in my heart I cannot hear
the whisper of your voice.

In the crashing of the water,
oh, speak to me, my God,
for in my soul I cannot feel
the flowing of your grace.

In the swelling of earth's seeds,
oh, speak to me, my God,
for in my world I cannot see
the bursting of your fruit.

Oh, speak to me, speak to me,
cry loud enough, my God,
that all creation round me birth
the glory of your face.

This Week:

Listen to
and observe
the natural world.

Week 8

We are to sink eternally
from letting go
to letting go
into God.
—MEISTER ECKHART

Often my life is like
a spinning top
hurtling through the days,
spinning,
spinning,
spinning,
savoring nothing,
threshing air and noise.
Then, suddenly,
unbalanced,
thrown,
my ground is gone
my dance is done,
slowly unwinding
I fall,
stunned,
stilled,
into the steady arms
of God.

This Week:

Pause.
Breathe deeply.

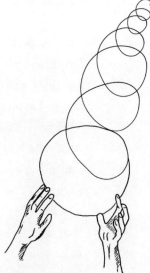

Week 9

I, God, am your playmate.
I will lead the child in you
in wonderful ways
for I have chosen you.

—MECHTILD OF MAGDEBURG

O God,
that we might dance
with you,
that we might rise
from heavy ground
and play with you
around around.
May we let go
of sterile fear
and jump as freely
as young deer.
O God,
that we might trust
your grace
and leap with joy
in your great embrace.

This Week:

Do something playful or ridiculous for God.
(You can do it in private.)

Week 10

I am ground of your prayers.
First,
it is my will that you have what you desire.
Later,
I cause you to want it.
Later on,
I cause you to pray for it, and you do so.
How then can you not have what you desire?
—JULIAN OF NORWICH

Often we anxiously seek the will of God,
as if God had gleefully hidden dreams for us
deep in unfathomable places.
As if it were God's intention
that our whole lives be spent
in endless searching for signs and directions
buried in obscurity.
The will of God is that which brings us
peace and fullness of life.
The will of God is the seed of our dreams
ever gestating with possibility
and longing to leap forward
scattering new and surprising blessings
in our gray reality.

This Week:

Identify a dream or hope
you have buried within you.
Hold it.
Befriend it.
Believe in it.

Week 11

Christ could be born
a thousand times in Galilee –
but all in vain
until he is born in me.

—ANGELUS SILESIUS

Seed of God,
be born in me,
thrust new-life forward
like a sap-filled tree
rising from
Your pool of grace
rooted in my womb's embrace.
Seed of God,
burst forth from me,
let me stretch
that God
might be.

This Week:

Stretch yourself
to live like Jesus.
Be Christ this week.

Week 12

Without forgiveness there is no future.
—ARCHBISHOP DESMOND TUTU

A young woman was put to death by lethal injection in Texas. She had murdered two people on a drug-crazed rampage. She was the daughter of a prostitute, smoked marijuana at eight, took cocaine at ten, and was forced into prostitution at fourteen by her mother.

After her arrest she spent over a dozen years on Death Row and during that time became a "born-again" Christian. Karla Faye Tucker found God, who had always been waiting for her, on Death Row. And Karla Faye found a deep joy she had never before experienced in life. Her eyes shone with God's love, and she asked forgiveness of her victim's families and pledged her life to one of reparation.

All her appeals failed, and she was executed by the State. Her last words asked for forgiveness and declared her love for those who were to witness her dying. She died praying.

As I watched the TV coverage of the killing, I felt a little of what must be God's pain at our frightening lack of mercy and compassion. For a woman whom I had never met I shed tears that night. In those tears I recognized and knew Karla Faye Tucker as my sister. And I came to understand, in that moment of anguish, that in the darkness hovering over our nation we had extinguished a light that God alone had lit. Our darkness has grown deeper. The mystical heart embraces all, loves all, forgives all.

This Week:

Do something to fight the death penalty, or hold in your heart and prayers the men and women who await execution on Death Row.

Week 13

The world is hungry for goodness
and recognizes it when it sees it. . . .
When we glimpse it in people we applaud them for it.
We long to be just a little like them.
Through them we let the world's pain into our hearts,
and we find compassion.

—ARCHBISHOP DESMOND TUTU

Oh, let us dare to be vulnerable!
Let us dare to believe that we are as capable
as Mother Teresa, Gandhi, Martin Luther King,
and even Jesus,
of acts of love and compassion!
But first we must be vulnerable.
We must acknowledge and accept
our own fear and insecurity
before the enormous task of transformation.
Yet still, in the face of God's grace,
we must cherish our possibilities.
It is then, from within our grace-filled trembling,
that we dare to step forward in trust and tenderness
to the brokenness of others.
God will transform our small hearts
into vessels of great grace.
We are capable of healing the world.

This Week:

Perform an act of compassion.

Week 14

God expects but one thing of you:
that you should come out of yourself
insofar as you are a created being
and let God be God in you.

— MEISTER ECKHART

In silence
we hear God's whisper
moving like a feather
through our being,
stroking and transforming
timid souls into
fiery passion
for justice.
In silence
God
finds voice
to cry aloud for
the little ones —
too broken and
too crushed
to speak aloud themselves.
In silence God cries.
And is heard.

This Week:

Be silent.
In that silence
allow God's grace
and God's voice
to rise from you
and speak in you.

Week 15

That which is impossible for you
is not impossible to me;
I will preserve my Word in all things
and I will make all things well.

—JULIAN OF NORWICH

I had a dream
which someone stole
and trampled all upon,
ripping my lovely rainbow
and scattering
its brilliant colors
upon the muddied floor.

Then moving within
my deep despair
God gently whispered low:
See these tiny pieces
scattered wide upon the floor?
I will rebuild them
bit by bit
to rise before your eyes
a kaleidoscope of beauty –
brilliant as sunrise.

This Week:

Give your pain,
your sense of failure and loss,
in trust to God.

Week 16

Never am I outside my God;
God is not outside of me.
I am God's radiance and God's light,
And God adorneth me.

—ANGELUS SILESIUS

We are each of us
a bit of God,
a scrap of divinity.
If we would know it,
Oh! if only
we could know it,
we would walk the earth
in awe,
eyes shining in splendor,
hearts suspended in delight
at the miracle
of the living God
gracing our days
and nights.

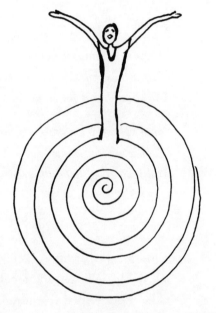

This Week:

Lie awake in the darkness one night.
Become conscious, for a few moments,
of the light within you.

Week 17

Some keep the Sabbath going to Church
I keep it staying at home –
With a bobolink for a chorister
And an orchard for a dome.

Some keep the Sabbath in surplice
I just wear my wings –
And instead of tolling the Bell for Church,
Our little Sexton sings.

—EMILY DICKINSON

God escaped from
all my little boxes and labels.
The more I tried to claim God,
the more God slipped away.
But if I dare
to rise from my knees
and leap in joy
at the song of the bird,
and if I dare
to stand in awe
at the mounting of the moon
in a thick-starred sky,
and if I dare to be amazed
at the constant seeding of the earth –

46

then, oh, see! oh, see!
I glimpse my God –
ever free, ever dancing,
ever calling out my name.

This Week:

**Stand before the moon
or listen to a bird.**

Week 18

Who would have ever thought of this:
that darkness brings forth light,
that light itself springs up from death,
a something out of naught.

—ANGELUS SILESIUS

Let me remember
when I no longer see
that You, sweet God,
hover close,
watching over me.
Let me remember
when I'm in deep despair
that You, sweet God,
hold me up
in ever tender care.
Let me remember
when I don't know where You are
that You, sweet God,
gestate in me
pin point, brilliant star.

This Week:

Sit in darkness for a while. Close your eyes.
Imagine God as a pin point of light
deep within you.

Week 19

In a season of calm weather
though inland far we be
our souls have sight of that immortal sea
which brought us hither.

—WILLIAM WORDSWORTH

If at any time or moment
in your life
you turned to God in yearning,
that moment is held by God
for all eternity —
jealously guarded
and kept in love.
Though it may dim and fade
from your awareness and memory
God, in delirious delight,
can never forget
nor let go
of that moment.
And God will wait,
longing,
for your return.

This Week:
Be comforted.

Week 20

Everything that is bathed in God
is enveloped by God,
who is round about us all,
enveloping us.

        — MECHTILD OF MAGDEBURG

The earth is shrouded
in a milky morning dew,
transparent,
yet obscuring
sharp lines
and blunt edges.
Everything is gentled.
The creeping light
wraps itself around
shapes and shadows,
enveloping all.
So does God's grace fall,
Her mighty maternal Spirit
pervading all our habitat,
stroking our darkened humanity
in urgent invitation
to gentleness
and new life.

This Week:

Be gentle with yourself.

Week 21

*Seeing his mother near the cross
and the disciple he loved standing near her,
Jesus said to his mother, "Woman, this is your son."
Then to the disciple he said, "This is your mother."*

—JOHN 19:25–27

My son, my son, my lovely son,
whence comes your hot hot rage?
Threshing violence, spitting pain
at such a tender age.

My son, my son, my lovely son,
how did terror first seize your heart?
Was it in the silence of the womb
that you were torn apart?

My son, my son, my lovely son,
I'll beat on heaven's door.
I'll rouse the hosts of angels
that you may sob no more.

My son, my son, my lovely son,
I'll leave nothing left undone.
I'll scour the earth for help, my son,
till your lonely hell is gone.

Editor's note: Edwina's son suffered from a prenatal condition, which has since been
successfully treated.

This Week:

Try not to judge another's anger.

Week 22

If there is a meaning in life at all,
then there must be a meaning in suffering.
Suffering is an ineradicable part of life,
even as fate and death.
Without suffering and death
human life cannot be complete.

—VICTOR E. FRANKL

Holy Spirit, Birthing Power,
stay with me
in this dark hour.
Holy Spirit, Wisdom's Breath,
warm me in
this creeping death.
Holy Spirit, Fierce light,
come burst upon
my inky night.
Holy Spirit, Brooding Dove,
seize me in
your hot, hot love.

This Week:

**Write a prayer
to the Holy Spirit.**

Week 23

All will be well,
and all will be well,
and every manner of thing
will be well.

—JULIAN OF NORWICH

I must take all
in trust,
though it seems
hell itself
assaults me.
I can never know
nor understand
what God does
or why.
I can only stand,
baffled, bruised,
even bleeding
and give it all over
to God,
all of it,
all of it,
to God
from whence
it came.

This Week:

Carry in your heart and mind
the words of Julian.

Week 24

We are incomparably stupid
when we do not strive to know who we are.
Seldom do we consider the precious things
that can be found in the soul
or who dwells in it or its high value. . . .
The soul is capable of much more
than we can imagine.

—TERESA OF AVILA

God loves us when we cannot;
God holds us when we will not;
God sees us when we dare not;
God knows us when we do not.

But, oh, that we might come
to love and hold ourselves,
to see and know ourselves,
that we might then glimpse God.

This Week:
Pray for self-knowledge
so that you might more clearly reflect God.

Week 25

God in heaven,
let me really feel my nothingness,
not in order to despair over it,
but in order to feel the more powerfully
the greatness of Thy Goodness.

—SØREN KIERKEGAARD

So far fallen!
Oh, gather me in,
my God,
Hold me tight
in your warm embrace;
grasp me in
your tender grace.
So far fallen!
Oh, speak Your love,
my God.
Dissolve my fear,
my darkened pain
in the whisper
of Your name.
So far fallen!
Raise me up,
my God.

Reach for me
from the stars above,
Oh, let me rest
in the Wings of the Dove.

This Week:

Let your God love you.

Week 26

Earth's crammed with heaven
and every common bush alive with God,
but only he who sees it takes off his shoes,
the rest sit round and pluck blackberries.
— ELIZABETH BARRETT BROWNING

I felt myself a tiny speck of life
standing, awed,
before God's creation.
I saw the vast sky meeting
the shining waters and, beyond,
clusters of trees huddling
in the folds of rolling hills.
The beauty stretched
into oblivion,
into God,
Who first breathed it into being.
And as I stood transfixed
before the mighty work
of our planet,
I knew
God breathed there still,
in every drop of water,
in every blade of grass,
and in every clump of earth.

Coursing through every tree
God's grace,
driven life force,
flowed
in endless longing to create.

This Week:
Take a walk in the natural world
and pay attention to it.

Week 27

*What a full and pregnant thing life is
when God is known;
and what a weary emptiness it is without God!
The river of God is full of water,
and God will moisten and fill
these parched hearts of ours,
out of the river of his own life.*

—THOMAS ERSKINE

The rain is falling
like millions of silver jewels
shining against
the black of the night
to be absorbed
by the thirsty soil.

May Your grace, O God,
fall upon
our dried humanity
unceasing.
May we absorb
Your moistness
that our dried up hearts
may rise and swell
to bursting.

This Week:

As you water your plants or flowers,
imagine God's grace watering your soul.

Week 28

No death has greatness
but that from which new life
can spring.
No life more vital
than that which from the death
of self takes wing.

—ANGELUS SILESIUS

I fell into the abyss,
hurtled down
from once firm ground,
watched the brilliant colors
of my life
fade and merge like
a dying mist,
heard the vibrant laughter
of friends gathered
dissolve into
distant echoes,
and felt the slipping away
of secure familiar places.
I fell into the abyss,
knowing nothing now,
holding nothing now,
being nothing now.

And as I lay desolate,
God, fiery love,
greeted me
in the void,
Shimmering.

This Week:

**Meditate on the fact that God can never,
will never, leave you.**

Week 29

God replied (to Mechtild):
I wish always to be your physician
bringing healing ointment for all your wounds.
—MECHTILD OF MAGDEBURG

I give to you, Holy One,
my tiredness when
the day is done.
I give to you my anxious fears,
the pent-up heart
that holds back tears.
I give to you, Living One,
unfinished work,
things left undone,
calls not answered,
memos piled high,
my sense of failure,
my stifled cry.
Oh, I give to You,
Compassionate One,
my life's little pieces,
my broken song.
I give to You, God of all grace,
this broken pot,
this empty space.

This Week:

Identify your hurts.
Imagine God as a physician.
Pray for healing.

Week 30

Apprehend God in all things,
for God is in all things.

—MEISTER ECKHART

I sit,
silent and prayerful,
inviting and longing
God to rise
within my soul.
The telephone rings –
loud,
jarring,
startling
my gentled spirit,
dissolving
my precious moment
of stolen solitude.
Then,
in the clumsy move
from prayer
to telephone,
I suddenly know
(though with less comfort)
that God
is in the ringing,

that God
is
the interruption.
I hasten
to reply.

This Week:

**When the telephone rings,
think of God.**

Week 31

Each of us inevitable,
Each of us limitless – each of us with his or her right
    upon the earth,
Each of us allow'd the eternal purports of the earth,
Each of us here as divinely as any is here.

— WALT WHITMAN

Precious in God's sight you are,
divinely made in God's delight,
endowed with beauty wove deep within,
brighter than the darkest sin.

Wondrous in God's sight you are,
though fallen deep, though fallen far,
still full-graced to reach the stars,
to break all chains and burst all bars.

Beloved in God's sight you are,
Whose laser vision probes the years,
Who knows the pain, the lonely fears,
and weeps before your hidden tears.

Claimed in God's sight you are,
Who jealously formed you of His seed.
None can claim your special place
or rob you of your given grace.

Free in God's sight you are,
to rise in rainbow'd glory,
to claim the God-light in your soul
and tell the world your story.

This Week:

**Reach out in healing and compassion
to those who are imprisoned
physically, mentally, or emotionally.**

This poem is written for the women of Cambridge Springs Correctional Facility, Pennsylvania, and is dedicated to all women who are incarcerated.

Week 32

There are times
when in order to keep ourselves
in existence at all
we simply have to sit back for a while
and do nothing.

—THOMAS MERTON

Oh, I would love to sit in holy places,
but I pick raisins off the floor,
and instead of wandering through the woods,
I'm wiping jelly off the door.

Oh, I would love to meditate
and take the time I need, they say,
but I'm intent on fixing train tracks
and blowing up bright balloons to play.

Oh, I would love to soak in silence,
suffused in God's refreshing grace,
but I must roar like a Mammy Lion
and leap around in fierce chase.

O Mother God, when I lament,
and long for a quiet and lovely space,
let me remember You're as close
as in any retreat or desert place.

O Mother God, midst all the chaos,
of cleaning house and playing ball,
whisper to me, tell my spirit
that you embrace and treasure it all.

This Week:

Embrace the reality of your life right now.
God is there.

Week 33

Faith is trusting in God's faithfulness
even when there is no sign
of God's faithfulness anywhere.
—HENRY FISCHER

Once, when I felt very alone and afraid, I found a small chipmunk that had been caught by two cats. They were playing with the tiny creature, rolling her around and throwing her up in the air. Horrified I rushed forward, shooed away the cats and held the trembling chipmunk in the palm of my hand tenderly. I felt great compassion for the little thing. As I moved to put her in a safe place — she bit me! When I moved faster she bit me again and drew blood. I was angry and frustrated that I could not communicate with the chipmunk to let her know that she was safe, that I held her in the palm of my hand, that I cared only to assure her that she would come to no harm. As I laid her in a safe place and observed her trembling, I thought of God.

God also holds us, like the trembling chipmunk, in the palm of God's hand and longs to comfort and reassure us. But often we are so bruised and afraid we find it hard to trust, to relax, to allow God to cradle us and carry us.

This Week:

Imagine you are the chipmunk.
Let God carry you.

Week 34

An old French sentence says,
"God works in moments."
We ask for long life,
but it is deep life or grand moments that signify.
Let the measure of time be spiritual, not mechanical.
Moments of insight, of fine personal relation,
a smile, a glance –
what ample borrowers of eternity they are!

—RALPH WALDO EMERSON

Each day is so full
of action, noise, and haste
that I miss you, God.
I allow you to get lost
in my clutter.
Oh, let me,
in the midst of it all,
discern a little spark
of Your Presence.
Let me,
in the dizziness of my days,
feel the brush
of Your grace
as I rush by You.

O God,
let me understand and rejoice
that You
ever shadow me –
longing to be known,
longing to be loved.
In a single grace-filled
moment.

This Week:

Waste a little time, consciously, for God.

Week 35

Those who hear the call of the Spirit
go forward even in sleep.

God is so close,
so intimate,
like a shadow
that cannot separate
itself from us.
When we dance,
God dances.
When we weep,
God weeps.
When we run,
God runs with us.
Whenever we say:
"It is enough,
I am weary
and can go no further,"
God tenderly sits
and waits with us
until we are renewed
and ready to continue
the journey.
God moves at our pace.

This Week:

Imagine God as your Shadow.
Close your eyes and converse with your Shadow.

Week 36

If we knew how much God loves us,
we should always be ready to receive
equally and with indifference from His hand
the sweet and the bitter.

— BROTHER LAWRENCE

I watched my soul friend,
my champion, my mentor,
slowly die of cancer.
Fleeing the dying,
I ran outside and paced
the frosted lawn,
crushing the dried grass
in despair and seeking
the face of God amidst
the season's dyings.
Inconsolable,
I cried aloud
for healing, for a miracle,
some sign from
a living God.
But I only heard
a gentle whispering
of the wind among
the naked bushes —

like God passing by,
stroking my great pain
with a velvet kiss –
but no promise.
Leaving me
loved,
but utterly, utterly
desolate.

This Week:

**Ask not to understand,
but to hold on in faith.**

Week 37

True prayer requires no word, no chant,
no gesture, and no sound.
It is communion, calm and still
with our own godly Ground.

—ANGELUS SILESIUS

Rest your bones in silence,
still your racing heart,
close your tired and restless eyes,
and come awhile apart.

Leave everything behind you,
come naked and bereft,
you will receive a hundredfold
of all that you have left.

Rest with God, beloved,
who waits for you alone,
to pause upon your journey
and stay with God at home.

Come swiftly, loved and precious one,
God longs to sit with you,
to absorb your lovely presence
as the flower holds the dew.

This Week:

Do it.

Week 38

We cannot take God by storm.
— THOMAS KELLY

I do not need
to pursue God.
I do not need
to chant and cry aloud.
I do not need
to seek out holy places,
blessed shrines
and holy signs.
I need only,
O God,
I need only
to whisper —
Yes.

This Week:

Whisper Yes.

Week 39

As the drop poured into the ocean is the ocean,
not the ocean the drop,
so the soul drawn into God is God,
not God the soul.
The soul is in God as God is in God.

—MEISTER ECKHART

Imagine an ocean,
and that you took a few drops from the ocean.
The drops would not be the ocean –
they would merely be drops of it,
of the same essence and substance as the ocean
but not the ocean itself.
In the same way we,
who burst forth from a passionate God
made in God's image and likeness,
are not God.
But we are little drops of God.
God-drops.
Polluted, muddied – yes.
Nevertheless, we are little drops of God
called to come together
in self-recognition and community.
To the degree that we do not recognize
God's presence in ourselves,

God is diminished in our world.
God's face will be revealed
when we recognize who we are
and claim and celebrate that reality.

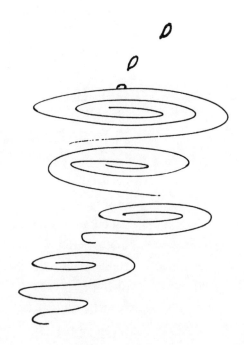

This Week:

Imagine yourself as a God-drop.
Whoever you meet this week,
try to see them and treat them
as a drop of God.

Week 40

God waits on human history
and suffers as She waits.

—MEISTER ECKHART

In the clutter
of my life
I left my God behind.
Until one day,
devastated
by a chaos
which all-enveloped me,
God stirred,
right in the middle
of it all.
And I knew
(deep joy)
that God
rested there –
ever –
in the heart
of my turmoil.

This Week:

**Allow yourself to stop
for a moment's silence
and feel God's stillness
in the center of your chaos.**

Week 41

Lo, soul, seest thou not God's purpose from the first?
The earth to be spann'd, connected by network,
The races, neighbors, to marry and be given in marriage,
The oceans to be cross'd, the distant brought near
The lands to be welded together.

—WALT WHITMAN

We build walls around our hearts, around our land, around our borders to keep out the strangers, the different, the other; to protect ourselves from getting hurt or from having to share our space with others. We guard our hearts, our land, and our country with great vigilance until the very guarding obsesses us and we become so outwardly focused and defensive that we lose touch with ourselves and our humanity. In our efforts to protect and defend we become disconnected and fragmented.

God, who will have nothing of walls and barriers, is like the Great Illegal Immigrant — ever looking for cracks in our walls and defenses, seeking vulnerability so that She might slip through our barriers to convert and to transform us. God, in great longing for wholeness, constantly invites us to dismantle all that is exclusive. We cannot be whole until we come to embrace all that God has made and to share all that God has given. In matters and issues of exclusion we may be sure that

God is always on the outside with those very people whom we do not accept. We diminish ourselves and we diminish God until we break down our walls. All of them.

This Week:

Identify a barrier,
a prejudice,
or discrimination in your life
which separates you
from your brother or sister.
Begin to dismantle it.

Week 42

The Holy Spirit is an unquenchable fire
Who bestows all excellence,
sparks all worth,
awakens all goodness,
ignites speech,
enflames humankind.

The Holy Spirit
through one's fervent longings
pours the juice of contrition
into the hardened human heart.

—HILDEGARD OF BINGEN

Break upon us, Holy One,
Your people are afraid
of muggings, rapes, and toxic bombs
of gun blasts and steel blades.

Break upon us, Holy One,
Your people sicken fast
from poisoned air and new diseases
and nature's furious blasts.

Break upon us, Holy One,
Your people wander lost

down paths of injustice and poverty
in pursuit of lowest cost.

Break upon us, Holy One,
send down Your Shining Dove,
embrace our over-crusted hearts
and melt them with Your Love.

This Week:
Identify both a personal
and a national sickness.
Pray for healing and conversion.

Week 43

I pray God to rid me of God.
—MEISTER ECKHART

Once, when I was preparing to spend a period of time in a hermitage I found myself spontaneously writing. The words tumbled from deep within me: "When I asked my God if I could come and stay with Him awhile, She said: Yes, but don't bring your God with you."

Oh, how easy it is to clutter up the path of the Holy Spirit with my images and preconceptions of God! The mystical heart lets go of all images, icons, and expectations of God. The mystical heart waits. Knowing nothing. Expecting nothing. The mystical heart is ever pregnant with the possibility of God. The mystical heart waits in awe for the revelation of God in every single moment.

O

This Week:

Clean out something in your home or office.
As you do this, ask God to help you
clean out the clutter within yourself.

Week 44

God hugs you.
You are encircled
by the arms
of the mystery of God.
　　　　　—HILDEGARD OF BINGEN

In a still, gray moment
in a quiet lonely place
may God's gentle mantle enfold you
and circle you with grace.
May Her sweet breath brush upon you
and warm your body through,
Her gracious arms encircle you
like a flower wrapped with dew.
May you truly know within
that you are God's delight,
and She longs to hold and love you
through your deep, deep night.

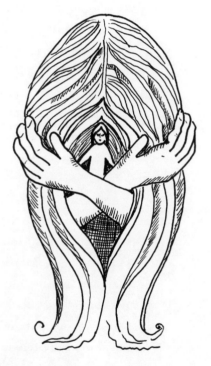

This Week:

Feel yourself encircled by God.
Sit quietly with this image whenever you can.

Week 45

I was hungry and you gave me food,
I was thirsty and you gave me drink,
I was a stranger and you made me welcome;
naked and you clothed me,
sick and you visited me,
in prison and you came to see me. . . .
I tell you solemnly,
insofar as you did this
to one of the least of my brothers and sisters,
you did it to me.

—JESUS OF NAZARETH

O living God, soften us!
Let the fire of Your love
thaw the frost within us.
Let the light of Your justice
sear away our blindness.
Let the grace of Your compassion
heal our hardened spirits.
O living God, soften us!
That, flowing with Your grace,
we be impelled to face the world
in bold compassion,
that, driven to justice,
we may dare to cry aloud

for the little ones,
the raped, the beaten,
the imprisoned, and the hungry.
O living God, soften us!
Sweep us forward
in a Mighty Wave of Mercy
to heal our darkened world.

This Week:

**Participate in some way
in a cause for justice.**

Week 46

No one listens, they tell me,
and so I listen . . .
and I tell them
what they have just told me,
and I sit in silence
listening to them,
letting them grieve.
        —JULIAN OF NORWICH

O God, ever vigilant
to the beating of my heart,
gather up the dreams
seeding in my soul,
listen to my words —
deep-felt but yet unformed,
longing to be uttered,
still waiting to be heard.
O God, gentle listener,
into Your bosom's warmth
absorb the silence of my song —
there to caress and
there to hold
till the fullness of its time.

This Week:

Listen deeply to someone.

Week 47

Everything can be taken from a person
but one thing;
the last of the human freedoms –
to choose one's attitude
in any given set of circumstances,
to choose one's own way.

—VICTOR E. FRANKL

O God,
let me not join the war cries
out of fear of being
unpatriotic.
Let me not remain silent
before the lethal injection
so not to look soft
on crime.
O God,
let me not point my finger
at those on welfare
so as to be embraced
by the righteous employed.
O God,
let me not avert my eyes
from poverty
so my security remains intact.

O God,
gentle, compassionate God,
bathe me
in Your grace
that I might stand my ground
before the Status Quo,
that I might speak Your truth
before the mighty machinery
of our bloodless political system.
O God, be born in me.
Change the world, O God,
in me.

This Week:

Make a conscious effort to become
politically aware, locally or nationally,
of issues and legislation
that adversely affect the poor.
Explore ways to make your voice heard.

Week 48

Once I am melted into God,
I will have then arrived
where I have been before I was
from all eternity.

—ANGELUS SILESIUS

Outside
the snow is melting,
breaking open
and collapsing
into spreading pools
that moisturize the earth.

So too
must I melt,
break open
my hardened heart
and collapse my closed mind
into open spaces
for tenderness
to take root.

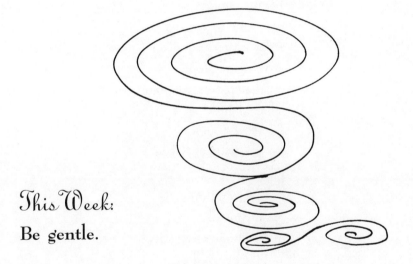

This Week:

Be gentle.

Week 49

*And 'tis my faith that every flower
enjoys the air it breathes.*

—WILLIAM WORDSWORTH

In my garden
early one winter day
I saw a tiny snowdrop
growing all alone
on the cold grassed lawn.
That night
the snow began to fall,
thick relentless flakes
piled up
two feet and more,
obscuring all
in blinding frozen white.
Winter dragged on
stunning all life
into silence.
Until, at last,
the thaw began,
and heavy mounds of snow
slowly caved
into icy puddles.

And then, amazed,
I saw standing
all alone
my tiny slender snowdrop
trembling in the wind —
firm, fragile, miraculous.
How did she live?
How did she stand
weighted down
so long and
knowing only darkness?
But there she was,
there she was,
smiling.

This Week:

Take a few moments to enter
into the image of the snowdrop.
Be the snowdrop.
Experience the heavy fall of snow,
the long darkness and the silence.
Then imagine the gradual thaw,
and feel yourself free, fragile, still.
Rooted.
Smile.

Week 50

I fled Him, down the nights and down the days;
I fled Him, down the arches of the years;
I fled Him, down the labyrinthine ways
Of my own mind; and in the midst of tears
I hid from Him, and under running laughter.
    Up vistaed hopes, I sped;
    And shot, precipitated,
Adown Titanic glooms of chasmed fears,
From those strong feet that followed, followed after.

—FRANCIS THOMPSON

O God, that I might cease to flee
Your clouds of mercy offered me,
that I might cease to spurn in fear
Your mighty grace that hovers near,
that I might come to turn around
and firmly walk on holy ground.
O God, that I might fall to rest
upon your loving waiting breast.

This Week:
Slow down.

Week 51

*It is as if I were the only person on the globe,
and God, too, were alone waiting for me.*
—ABRAHAM JOSHUA HESCHEL

Still, beloved,
gentle now.
All is gathered
in My arms.
All things happen
beneath My gaze.
Nothing is
that is not Me.
Peace, beloved,
sink in Me,
Who hold all life
in infinity.
Trust, beloved,
all's meant to be
in your unfolding
from eternity.
Still, beloved,
quiet be.
Come, My love,
and sleep in Me.

This Week:

Take some time off, treat yourself,
and get a good night's sleep.

Week 52

All created things are but the crumbs which fall from the table of God.

— ST. JOHN OF THE CROSS

God

is

BIG.

This Week:

Just imagine that!

Of Related Interest

Marsha Sinetar
HOLY WORK
Be Love. Be Blessed. Be a Blessing.

The bestselling author of *Do What You Love, the Money Will Follow*
shows us how to be a blessing in our daily work and to appreciate
the blessings that follow. A year's worth of weekly meditations
followed by Scripture verses and stimulating questions for reflection.

0-8245-1759-8; $19.95

Frank X. Tuoti
WHY NOT BE A MYSTIC?

An irresistible invitation to know the presence of God –
here and now.

0-8245-1453-X; $12.95

Anthony J. Ciorra
EVERYDAY MYSTICISM
Cherishing the Holy

"Creative and practical – a contemporary spirituality for life in the
messy market place." - Joseph M. Champlin

0-8245-1483-1; $14.95

Please support your local bookstore, or call 1-800-395-0690.
For a free catalog, please write us at
THE CROSSROAD PUBLISHING COMPANY
370 LEXINGTON AVENUE, NEW YORK, NY 10017

We hope you enjoyed A Mystical Heart. *Thank you for reading it.*

crossroad